IT'S SCIENCE!

Food

Sally Hewitt

CHILDREN'S PRESS®

A Division of Grolier Publishing

NEW YORK • LONDON • HONG KONG • SYDNEY
DANBURY, CONNECTICUT

Acknowledgments:
Cover: Steve Shott; Bruce Coleman pp. 14tl (Harald Lange), 16tm (Gerald Cubitt), 26bl (Kevin Rushby); FLPA pp.
26tl (Philip Perry), 26tr (D. P. Wilson); Holt Studios International pp. 7l (Nigel Cattlin), 14tm (Nigel Cattlin), 14tr (Nigel Cattlin)
14bl (Nigel Cattlin), 16tr (Gordon Roberts), 17tl (Nigel Cattlin), 17tr (Nigel Cattlin); Images Colour Library pp. 15tl, 25tr;
Planet Earth Pictures p. 7m (Martin Rugner), 16br (Peter J. Oxford); Telegraph Colour Library p. 7r (Frank Krahmer).
Thanks, too, to our models: Shauna Morris, Natimi & Shalika Black-Heaven, Jack Mitchell and Erin Bhogal.

Series editor: Rachel Cooke
Designer: Mo Choy
Consultant: Sally Nankivell-Aston
Picture research: Sue Mennell
Photography: Ray Moller unless otherwise acknowledged

First published in 1999 by Franklin Watts
96 Leonard Street, London EC2A 4XD

First American edition 2000 by Children's Press
A division of Grolier Publishing
90 Sherman Turnpike, Danbury, CT 06816

Visit Children's Press on the Internet at:
http://publishing.grolier.com

Hewitt, Sally
    Food / Sally Hewitt.
        p. cm. -- (It's science!)
        Summary: Discusses the different food groups, what kinds of food
    they contain, their sources, and their nutritional value.
        ISBN 0-516-21653-8
        1. Food Juvenile literature. [1. Food.] I. Title. II. Series:
    Hewitt, Sally. It's science!
    TX355.H485 2000
    641.3--dc21   99-21141
                                                        CIP

GROLIER
PUBLISHING

Contents

Food for Life

Plants, animals, and everything that is alive, including you, need food. Food gives your body the **energy** to work, keep warm, and stay healthy.

You are still growing. Food gives your body the goodness it needs to grow skin, muscles, and bone.

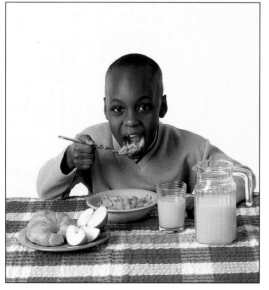

After a night's sleep or when you have been playing or working hard and you haven't eaten for a while, you feel hungry. Your **stomach** is empty and you need food.

TRY IT OUT!

Start the day with a good breakfast. It will give you the energy you need for all the things you want to do before lunch.

6

Plants make their own food. They change the heat energy in sunlight into food in their green leaves.

Rabbits eat plants such as grass and vegetables. They are hunted and eaten by meat eaters.

Foxes are meat eaters. They hunt and eat other animals such as rabbits that eat plants.

Follow this **food chain**. You can see that even though foxes don't eat plants, they would soon go hungry if there were no plants for rabbits to eat.

THINK ABOUT IT!

Where do you think people would fit in a food chain?

Eating

You have to eat food to get the energy and goodness from it.

Before you start eating, the smell of food you like makes your mouth water as it fills with **saliva**.

You chew your food into small pieces. Saliva helps your food slip down when you swallow and starts to break up the food even more.

You need strong, healthy teeth to eat your food. Food left around your teeth can damage them, particularly if it is sugary — so brush your teeth every morning and evening to keep them clean.

The food you have chewed goes into your stomach, where juices break it down into smaller pieces.

Then the food goes into a long tube called the **small intestine**, where juices break it down again to pass the goodness from the food to the rest of your body.

Your body gets rid of the unused parts of food when you go to the toilet.

This breaking up of food in your body is called your **digestion**.

THINK ABOUT IT!

What food do you enjoy eating?
Why do you like it so much?

Good Food

There are four main groups of food. Eating a good variety from each group every day helps keep you strong and healthy.

You need only a small amount of **fat** for warmth and energy.

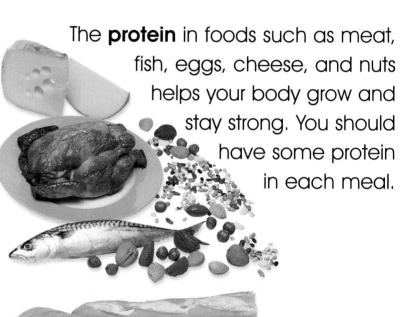

The **protein** in foods such as meat, fish, eggs, cheese, and nuts helps your body grow and stay strong. You should have some protein in each meal.

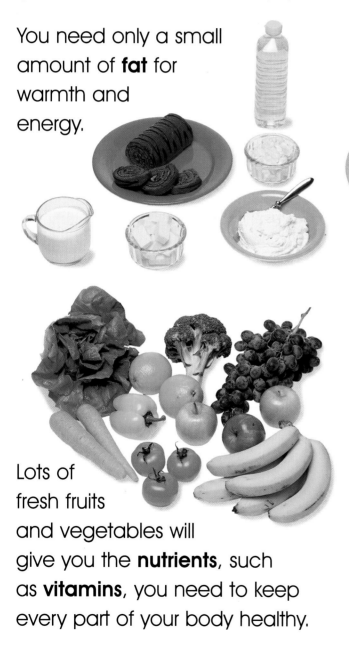

Lots of fresh fruits and vegetables will give you the **nutrients**, such as **vitamins**, you need to keep every part of your body healthy.

The **carbohydrates** in this group of food give you energy. Plenty of bread, pasta, rice, or potatoes will help keep you going.

Snacks such as chips and chocolate are full of salt and sugar, and too much of them is not good for you. Try an apple and some raisins for a snack instead.

Your body also needs a lot of water to work properly, so don't forget to drink water as well as eat good food.

TRY IT OUT!

Plan a meal you would like to eat, choosing food from all the four groups. Is it a healthy meal?

Is this meal full of the goodness you need?

Fruits and Vegetables

The fruits and vegetables we eat are all parts of plants. Fruit is the part of a plant that holds the **seeds**.

Sweet pineapples, bananas, and melons are all fruits. So are apples and pears.

Some fruits are not sweet, such as tomatoes and zucchini. We often call these fruits vegetables, but can you spot the seeds that show they are fruits?

Vitamins and **minerals** are found in most foods but fruits and vegetables give us the most. Oranges are full of vitamin C. It keeps your skin healthy and helps make you better when you are sick.

The vegetables we eat can come from all different parts of a plant.

Broccoli is a kind of flower.

We eat the leaves of lettuce.

Crunchy celery is a stalk.

Carrots are roots growing under the earth.

 THINK ABOUT IT!

What parts of the plants do you think potatoes, cauliflower, cabbage, onions, and spinach come from?

 TRY IT OUT!

Ask an adult to help you wash and slice some fresh fruits or vegetables to make a fruit salad or a vegetable salad that is good to eat.

13

Grains

Grains are seeds. Grains we can eat are used to make a lot of our food. You probably eat some kind of grain every day.

This is barley.

This is corn.

These are oats.

Wheat is a kind of grain that gives food for millions of people all over the world. It is grown in huge fields that stretch as far as you can see.

Grains of wheat are ground into a powder called flour, which is used to bake all these different things to eat.

Rice is another important grain. It grows in hot places underwater in flooded paddy fields.

The food made from grains is full of **fiber**. We sometimes call it **roughage**. There is roughage in fruits and vegetables, too.

Roughage helps all the food you eat pass through your body more easily.

Can you tell which of these foods are good to eat for roughage?

LOOK AGAIN

Look again at page 10 to find which group of food grains belong to.

Food from Animals

Some of the food we eat comes from animals. It gives us protein, fat, minerals and vitamins.

Cattle, sheep, and pigs are farmed for meat.

Fishermen drop nets into the sea and pull up huge catches of fish. Sometimes fish are frozen on board ship as soon as they are caught, to keep them fresh.

💡 THINK ABOUT IT!

Some people choose not to eat meat and fish. Look at page 10. What could you have for protein instead of meat and fish?

Chickens give us eggs as well as meat.

Dairy cows are farmed for their milk. Milk is used to make all these different kinds of food.

TRY IT OUT!

Make some pancakes.
Pour 1 1/2 cups of plain flour into a bowl. Gradually whisk in 2 eggs and 1 1/4 cups of milk.
Ask an adult to help you to cook the pancakes.
You can eat your pancakes with syrup, butter, or anything you choose.

17

Pizza

Pizza is full of nutrients. Do you know where all the different kinds of food, or **ingredients**, used to make pizza come from?

A tomato is a fruit that turns red in the sunshine. Tomato sauce is made from crushed tomatoes.

Olives are the fruit of an olive tree. Olive oil is made from pressed olives.

Cheese is made from milk that comes from dairy cows.

Basil is an herb, which is a type of plant. Its leaves have a strong smell and taste.

Dough is made from flour, yeast, and water.

Yeast is a kind of fungus that is good for us. It makes the pizza dough rise.

Pepperoni is made from meat that has been ground up and forced into a sausage skin.

LOOK AGAIN

Look again at page 10. Which food groups do the ingredients of this pizza come from?

TRY IT OUT!

Make a pizza collage. Draw a large circle on a piece of cardboard and cut it out. Paint on red tomato sauce. Cut strips of yellow tissue paper for grated cheese. Cut circles of colored paper for pepperoni. Draw mushrooms and peppers and cut them out. Stick the things you have made on your pizza.

What else could you put on your pizza? Ask an adult to help you make a real pizza using the toppings you have chosen.

Look, Smell, and Taste

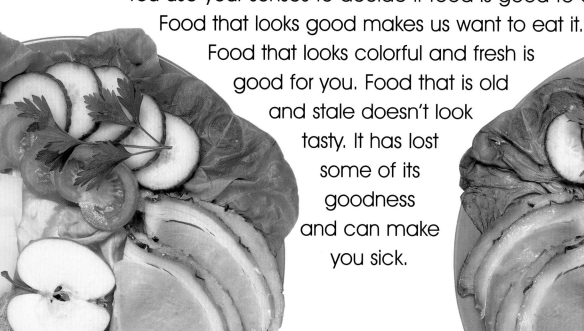

You use your senses to decide if food is good to eat.
Food that looks good makes us want to eat it.
Food that looks colorful and fresh is
good for you. Food that is old
and stale doesn't look
tasty. It has lost
some of its
goodness
and can make
you sick.

Which plate of food
would you rather eat?

 TRY IT OUT!

Make a meal that looks good to eat from
food that you don't need to cook. How
can you make it look even more delicious?

Uncooked food that smells nasty could be going bad. It might make you sick if you eat it.

The smell of good food cooking helps make you hungry. Just the smell can make your mouth water. This means your mouth is getting ready to eat the food.

Your tongue can detect only salty, sweet, sour, or bitter tastes. Has Anna just tasted something sweet or sour?

Salt, pepper, herbs, and spices are used to add flavor to food. You only need to use a little, as they have very strong tastes.

Chillies can make food taste very hot!

Fresh and Clean

Fresh food is good to eat, but food that has not been kept fresh can carry **germs** that can make you sick. Food can be kept fresh in different ways.

Fresh food such as green vegetables and fish can be kept in the refrigerator for several days. If you freeze it, it can be kept for several months.

Dried food keeps until water is added.

Food in a can keeps until the can is opened and air is let in.

Often food you buy has a "use by" date on its packaging. It tells you how long you can safely keep the food before eating it.

USE BY
1/1/2002

Good cooks make sure their food is fresh and everything they use is clean. Cooks often wear a hat to keep their hair out of the food.

Always wash your hands. They may have germs on them that could get into the food.

Wash your cooking utensils and dry them with a clean cloth.

Wash your hands

👁 LOOK AGAIN

Not all food has a date on it. Look at pages 20 and 21 to find other ways you can tell when food is not fresh.

 ## TRY IT OUT!

Make a poster to put in the kitchen to remind everyone about using fresh food and keeping clean.

23

Cooking

Most of the food we eat is cooked — it is heated until it changes. Raw food has not been cooked at all.

Cooking food makes it easier to chew and to break up inside your body. The heat also kills off germs and makes the food safe to eat.

Some foods taste much better cooked. Some are more tasty if they are raw.

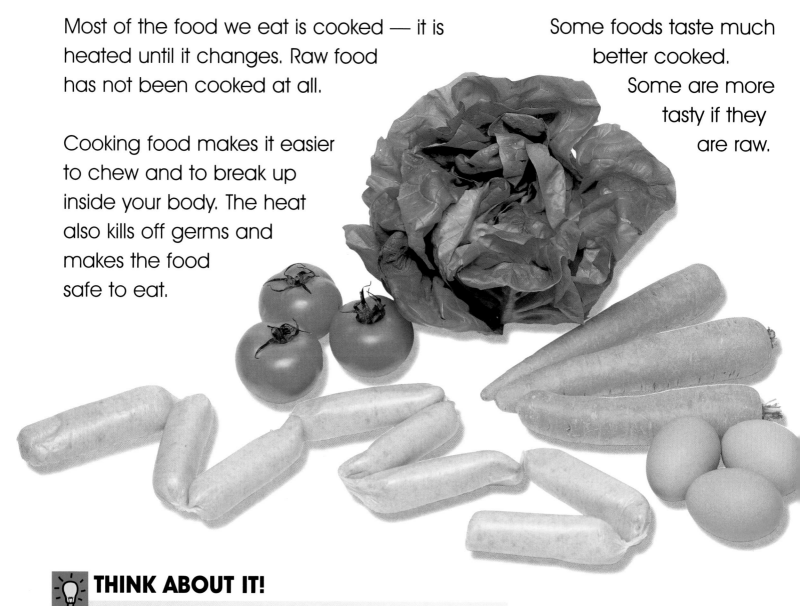

💡 **THINK ABOUT IT!**

Which of these foods could we eat raw?
What other foods can you eat raw?

24

The heat from a stove, a barbecue, or a fire is used for cooking food. We can use the heat to boil food in water, grill it, fry it in fat or oil, or bake it in an oven.

We fry or grill sausages. They look very different when they have been cooked.

Boiling, scrambling, and frying are different ways of cooking eggs. How was this egg cooked?

LOOK AGAIN

Look again at page 15 to see how boiling rice changes it. Does it get bigger or smaller?

Bread is baked in the oven. Flour, water, and yeast are the ingredients needed for making bread. Look how cooking changes bread dough.

Shopping

Do you like shopping for food? The food you buy comes from all over the world.

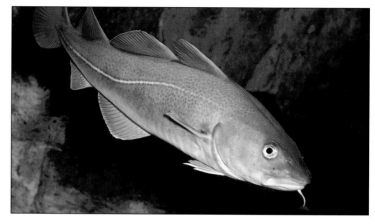

Bananas grow where it is hot and wet. Because they are sent to your store from far away, they are picked when they are still green. By the time they reach the stores, they are ripe and ready to eat.

The cod in your fish sticks is caught in cold seas and frozen on board ship to keep it fresh for you to buy.

Most of the tea we drink comes from India, where tea leaves are picked, dried, and put into packets.

 TRY IT OUT!

Look at the packaging and labels of the food in your cupboard or refrigerator and see if they tell you where it comes from.

The food from this shopping basket has been sorted into packets, cans, fresh food, and frozen food.

Now it has been sorted into food containing grains, fruits and vegetables, protein, and fat.

 THINK ABOUT IT!

What other ways can you think of for sorting this basket of food? Try sorting the food you buy into different groups next time you go shopping.

Useful Words

Carbohydrates Carbohydrates are found in some foods, such as bread and pasta. They help give you the energy you need each day.

Digestion The ways your body breaks down and uses the food you eat.

Energy Energy is what people, animals, and machines need to give them the power to do work. Your energy comes from food.

Fat There is fat in food such as meat and butter. Your body can store fat and use it slowly to give you energy.

Fiber Fiber is a part of plants, including food such as grains and vegetables. It helps food pass through your body easily.

Food chain A food chain is the name given to the link among plants and animals that is based on what they eat.

Germs Germs are too tiny to see with our eyes. They carry diseases that can make you feel sick. There may be germs in food that is not kept fresh.

Grains The seeds of plants such as wheat, barley, and corn are called grain. Grains can be dried and ground into flour. Bread and pasta are made from grains.

Ingredients Ingredients are the different foods we put together when we cook. For example, the ingredients for making pancakes are flour, eggs, and milk.

Minerals Tiny amounts of minerals are found in food. They are an important part of the goodness in food that helps keep you healthy.

Nutrients Nutrients are the goodness in food that you need to stay healthy.

Protein Protein in food such as fish, meat, eggs, and cheese helps build up strong bones and muscles in your body and helps it heal.

Roughage Roughage is another word for fiber in food. It helps food pass easily through your body.

Saliva Saliva is a liquid made in your mouth that helps your food slip down when you swallow. It starts to break up the food before it reaches your stomach.

Seeds Plants grow from seeds. A seed contains a new plant and its store of food.

Small intestine Food goes into your small intestine from your stomach. It is a long tube where juices continue to break down food from your stomach.

Stomach When you eat, the food goes into your stomach, where juices break it down into very small pieces.

Vitamins Vitamins are part of the goodness in food. They help keep every part of your body healthy.

Yeast Yeast is a tiny fungus used in baking. (Fungi are a group of living things, including mushrooms.) A mixture of water, sugar, and yeast added to bread dough makes it rise.

29

Index

About This Book

Children are natural scientists. They learn by touching and feeling, noticing, asking questions, and trying things out for themselves. The books in the *It's Science!* series are designed for the way children learn. Familiar objects are used as starting points for further learning. *Food* starts by asking why we need food and explores the different aspects of food that relate to science.

Each double page spread introduces a new topic, such as cooking food. Information is given, questions asked, and activities suggested that encourage children to make discoveries and develop new ideas for themselves.
Look for these panels throughout the book:

TRY IT OUT! indicates a simple activity, using safe materials, that proves or explores a point.
THINK ABOUT IT! indicates a question inspired by the information on the page but that points the reader to areas not covered by the book.
LOOK AGAIN introduces a cross-referencing activity that links themes and facts through the book.

Encourage children not to take the familiar world for granted. Point things out, ask questions, and enjoy making scientific discoveries together.